PRESENTED BY

a Friend

SMYTHE
GAMBRELL
LIBRARY

WESTMINSTER SCHOOLS

chris Leslie

A New True Book

MATTER

By Fred Wilkin

CHILDRENS PRESS ®

CHICAGO

Young girl holds two examples of matter—a fluid and a solid.

PHOTO CREDITS

Tony Freeman Photographs—38

Journalism Services:
© Joseph Jacobson—6, 12 (left)
© David Waselle—28 (left), 34 (right)
© Scott Wanner—28 (right)
© Mark Gamba—32

NASA-cover, 2, 30 (left), 34 (left)

Nawrocki Stock Photo:
© Jim Wright—2, 13 (right), 14, 15, 16 (left), 25, 26, 27, 40
© Wm. S. Nawrocki—8 (right), 24 (left), 37
© Michael Brohm—13 (left)
© Jim Whitmer—16 (right), 21
© Candee—24 (right), 36
© Frank Neiman—30 (right)
© Ken Sexton—35
© Jeff Apoian—39
© Carlos Vergara—45

Fred Wilkin—8 (left), 11, 12 (right), 19 (2 photos), 22, 23, 43

Library of Congress Cataloging-in-Publication Data

Wilkin, Fred
    Matter.

    (A New true book)
    Includes index.
    Summary: Discusses the properties of matter and presents several experiments demonstrating them.
    1. Matter—Properties—Juvenile literature.
[1. Matter—Properties] I. Title.
QC173.36.W55 1986   530   85-30882
ISBN 0-516-01284-3

TABLE OF CONTENTS

ALL THE MATTER
IN THE WORLD

From space, we see our planet earth. It has a round shape. It has certain colors.

That's about all anyone can tell about the earth from space. One could not tell what forms of matter make up this planet.

Air, water, and rocks are different forms of matter.

On solid earth, you can see different forms of matter. You breathe air, drink water, and eat foods. Gases (like air), liquids (like water), and solid substances (like food), are all forms of matter.

THE EARTH AND ITS MATTER

This planet, our world with its matter and the energy of the sun that shines upon it, provides what we need to live.

You don't have to think about matter in order to be alive. Plants and animals are living things. They are made up of matter, but they have no thoughts about matter itself.

Turtles (above) are living things, but only humans can think or reason.

Human beings are made up of matter, too. But they ask questions, look closely at things, and wonder. Humans get to know things about their world. It matters to them. It should matter to you.

There are really three things to talk about in our world: 1. Matter

        2. Space

        3. Energy

All three differ greatly, but in some ways a scientist could relate them all to each other.

All of the earth is matter, taking up the space it does. And energy is basic to what goes on everywhere on earth.

KINDS OF MATTER

It might seem that many kinds of matter make up our planet because of all the different kinds of things we know about. Humans have many names for these different things.

But only two words fit just about every kind of matter that there is.

One word for matter is *solid.* The other word for matter is *fluid.*

WHAT ABOUT SOLIDS?

Solid matter has a shape. Solid things stay as they are. Solids stay put. Pick up something solid. You can hold it, and it stays the same. You set it down someplace, it stays.

This stack of firewood is an example of a solid.

Electromagnet (left), attached to a crane, is a solid. The fossil fern (above) is a solid.

It keeps its shape. It takes up a certain amount of space.

You don't need a box or bottle to keep a solid together. You can pile up one kind of solid with other kinds of solids. Gravity will keep them in place.

A bulldozer (left) can move huge amounts of solid earth.
A knife (right) cuts solids into pieces.

Solids can be moved.
Sometimes they can be
broken into little chunks.
Some solids can be cut
with a solid knife or saw.
Some solids split. Some
bend or bounce.

Solids are what make up
the crusty surface of the

The plastic bag is a solid. When filled with water, it will take a different shape.

earth. We live mainly on the earth's surface of rock and soil. Everything rests on the surface in some way.

One thing is certain: solids don't change or do anything by themselves. They simply stay put until humans or forces or energy work on them.

Water is a fluid. It will take shape only when held in a container of some kind.

WHAT ABOUT FLUIDS?

Fluid matter doesn't stay put very well. It will keep to a particular shape only if it is in some form of container, such as a basin or bowl, a bottle or bag.

A fluid is any kind of

Gravity pulls fluids down. When you suck on
a straw (right), you overcome the pull of
gravity and can pull fluids up.

matter that flows. You have
trouble holding and picking
up a fluid without a
container. You can cup
your hands. You can suck
fluids through a straw.
Fluids flow and spread out.
Gravity pulls fluids down
to wherever they will flow.

Fluid matter covers the surface of the earth. Photographs from space show clouds and currents. They form a flowing, changing layer of fluid matter, going every which way.

The planet we live on has a thin coating of matter that is fluid.

One thing is certain: fluids will change only when forces or energy act on the kind of matter they happen to be. Then fluids can do some funny things.

ONLY TWO KINDS
OF MATTER

Solids and fluids are the only kinds of matter. But what about gases?

The fluids we see, feel, and study the most are the gas (air) and the liquid (water). Both air and water are fluid matter that share certain fluid properties. Gases and liquids are both fluids!

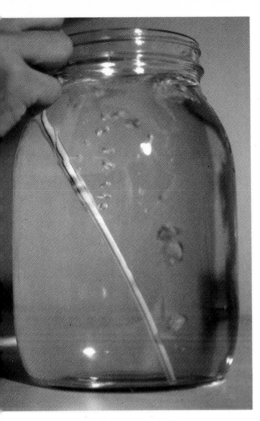

Water (left) surrounds the bubbles of air.
In the spill (above), air surrounds the
bubbles of water.

We can see a bubble of
air in water. We can see a
droplet of water in air. It's
a reverse! The water in
one case surrounds the air.
The air in the other case
surrounds the water. The

droplet of water will sink through the air, and the bubble of air will rise through the water.

In a way, a tiny bit of air in water and a tiny bit of water in air each will take a shape. Liquid fluid matter has a property that causes it to take a beady, round shape. But gas fluid matter won't do this by itself. It comes apart and spreads out if not contained.

IMPORTANT FLUID SAMENESSES

There are ways that liquids and gases are the same in order to be called fluids.

A hose or pipe works to get gases and liquids from one place to another. A

Freon, a heavy gas, is poured from one beaker to another.

pump will make both kinds of fluid move.

You can pour a liquid like water from a tumbler into another container.

This same kind of pouring can be seen if you pick Freon, a heavy gas, and pour it from a beaker

When Freon is poured into the box on the left the balance will tip to the left. Freon is heavier than air.

into another beaker. A jar containing Freon is heavier than a jar containing ordinary air. This would show on a scale.

Pouring a light gas like helium would work upside down. An upside down tumbler would "hold" the

Hot air balloons (left) and blimps (above) use helium, a gas that is lighter than air.

helium and, when tilted, would pour *up* into another container above it.

So liquids and gases can pour and even squirt. They are fluids. They adjust to the space they occupy. They take on the shape of the space they occupy.

A young scientist
squeezes air out of
an empty soda bottle.
Fluid air can be
squeezed.

IMPORTANT FLUID
DIFFERENCES

Gases and liquids take
up a certain amount of
space. A plastic soda pop
bottle isn't really empty
after you pour out the
soda. It has air inside. Air
is a gas. With the cap
screwed back on tightly,

you can squeeze the bottle and the air will squeeze. It is springy. Gases can be compressed.

Fill up the same bottle with water. Fill it all the way so that only liquid is inside when it is capped. It can't be squeezed. Liquids do not compress, or only

Fluid liquids cannot be squeezed, or compressed.

Bicycle pump forces air into a tire.

such a slight bit that you can hardly notice it.

This is a difference between gases and liquids. Some gas fluid matter can be pumped and packed so that lots and lots of it will squeeze into a container. A

Scuba tank (above) and oxygen tank (right)
hold fluid gas under pressure.

bike tire or a scuba tank
holds air under high
pressure. The volume of a
fluid gas can change.

A water tank, filled to
the top, cannot hold any
more water. Liquids keep
their same volume.

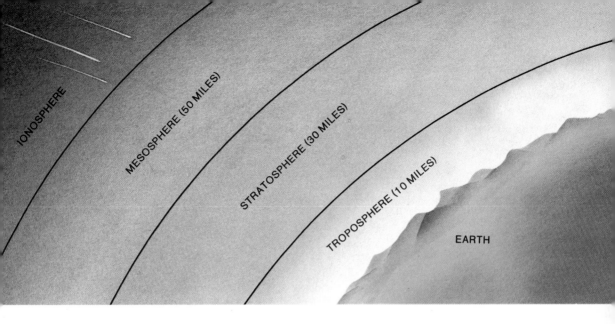

IONOSPHERE

MESOSPHERE (50 MILES)

STRATOSPHERE (30 MILES)

TROPOSPHERE (10 MILES)

EARTH

THE FLUID GASES AND LIQUIDS THAT COVER EARTH

The gases of our atmosphere are spread rather deeply all over the world. The atmosphere of fluid gases is from sixty to one hundred miles deep.

The ultralight plane (above) must cut through the fluid atmosphere that surrounds the earth. The space shuttle (left) flies above this fluid blanket.

Solid airplanes fly through this form of matter up to around five miles high. Gases are thinner as you go up.

Above this fluid atmosphere, at over one hundred miles, spacecraft, shuttles, and satellites stay in orbit without running through any fluid that would slow them down.

The fluid atmosphere is kept near and pressing down on the earth by gravity. While it is pressing down tightly upon us, we are living at the bottom of an ocean of air. This ocean of atmosphere is very important. It is the superfluid that we live in.

The water we see spread over the earth's surface fills ocean basins,

Iguazu Falls is a dramatic example of water seeking its lowest level.

trenches, rivers, lakes, and streams. Sometimes it is flowing. All the while, this liquid—water—is seeking its lowest level.

We see the fluid property of water quite clearly. In fact, most people might think of fluid matter only as water.

Water covers three-fourths of our planet. The solid crust under everything gives us something to stand on. Our fluid atmosphere totally surrounds the earth.

Humans must breathe air. In foreign environments, such as the moon (left) or beneath the oceans (right), humans must carry oxygen with them in order to survive.

You could not live without air. You would not be alive without water. These are certainly important fluid matters.

THE MATTER OF EATING

A plant is matter that sprouts with moisture, grows with energy from the sun, combines liquid and gas fluids with minerals that were solids, and sometimes is harvested for food. You

Plants grow using the energy from the sun and the minerals and moisture from the earth.

could not do any of the things a plant does with matter to survive by yourself. Plant matter, and what it does with matter, is basic to all life. The sun supplies the energy.

Animals eat plants in order to get energy for movement and growth that

Cows eat plants and grow.

People eat plants and animals.

they cannot produce for themselves. Then plant matter becomes animal matter.

Humans eat vegetables and meats and other forms of matter that have lived. Unlike plants, humans cannot make their own food.

Everything in the world is made up of matter of one kind or another.

THE MATTER OF PLANTS

What about a cotton shirt, a straw hat, and a baseball bat? Your own ideas of what comes from plants will add up when you look around at furniture, wooden houses, and the paper pages of a book. Even ink!

Animals give humans many things besides food.

THE MATTER OF ANIMALS

There are leather belts and shoes. Shells are made into buttons. Shark teeth might make a nifty necklace. Saddles for horses are a big item. How long a list can you come up with for animal products? Did you think of ivory toothpicks made from elephant tusks?

MATTERS OF INTEREST

What forms of matter make up the things that you are? Tap your teeth, pull your hair, and look at your fingernails. Pinch yourself somewhere. Feel your elbow. Wipe your nose.

Such a marvelous collection of matter you are. You are mostly water. You have iron in your blood along with oxygen

Humans are made up of gases, liquids, and solids.

from the air. You have
bones made of calcium.
Your skin and muscles are
very complicated
substances, a combination
of matter that has
managed to arrange itself
the way you are.

You are able to do that
without much action on the
part of your brain. You
grew. You are matter, but
a very special type. You
can look around at the
world you live on to see
how matter works.

When you look at the
world up close, you are
studying matter and its
interesting interactions.
Matter is all around you.

You should be able to
come up with more things
to wonder about that really
matter.

WORDS YOU SHOULD KNOW

animal(AN • ih • mil) — a special collection of matter that can move and respond to stimuli

atmosphere(AT • muss • feer) — the fluid gases that surround the planet earth

compress(kum • PRESS) — to press or squeeze together

curious(KYUR • ee • us) — interested in what is going on; inquisitive; wanting to learn

energy(EN • ur • jee) — natural power; the active power of doing work

fluid(FLOO • id) — a thing that takes the shape of its container, that flows and levels out, and that changes only when a force acts on it

gas(GAS) — a type of fluid that spreads out if not contained but that can be compressed

liquid(LICK • wid) — a type of fluid that flows to adjust to the space it occupies, that cannot be compressed, and that seeks its lowest level

matter(MAT • er) — material (solids and fluids) that takes up space and has weight; everything in existence except empty space

plant(PLANT) — matter that grows with energy from the sun and provides energy to animals and humans that eat it

solid(SOL • id) — a thing with a shape that takes up a certain amount of space and does not change or move until an outside force works on it

space(SPAISS) — absolutely nothing; what exists wherever matter happens not to be

INDEX

About the author

Fred Wilkin, Jr. is the Chairman of Natural Science at National College of Education. He has written scripts and acted as science consultant for a number of films and film strips on natural phenomena for Journal Films and SVE. Dr. Wilkin also has written science investigations for Ginn's science programs for grades 1 through 8.